The Cross in Your Path

Christian Books Publishing House
Jacksonville, FL

www.seedsowers.com

**By Sonny Bradley
and Gene Edwards**

The Cross in Your Path

Copyright © 2024 by John Bradley and Cindy J. Edwards

All rights reserved. No part of this publication may be reproduced, distributed, or transmitted in any form or by any means without prior written permission.

Seedsowers Publishing
Christian Books Publishing House, Inc.
3545 St Johns Bluff Rd S
Jacksonville, FL 32224
www.seedsowers.com

ISBN: 978-1-950891-03-0

Cover Photo by Clément Rémond on Unsplash

All Scripture is from the New American Standard Bible, copyright The Lockman Foundation

The Cross in Your Path / Sonny Bradley and Gene Edwards -- 1st ed.

To that cloud of witnesses who have gone before us bearing the cross.

CONTENTS

CHAPTER 1	The Way of the Cross	1
CHAPTER 2	Rebekah	7
CHAPTER 3	Job	15
CHAPTER 4	Paul	29
CHAPTER 5	Lazarus, Mary, and Martha	39
CHAPTER 6	The Ark	51
CHAPTER 7	Entitlement	59
CHAPTER 8	Consecration	65
CHAPTER 9	Success and Failure	69
CHAPTER 10	Decentralization	77
CHAPTER 11	His Cross at Gethsemane	85
CHAPTER 12	Betrayal	87
CHAPTER 13	Forgiveness	93
CHAPTER 14	Before the Collision	97
CHAPTER 15	Leaders	101
CHAPTER 16	Division in the Body of Christ	105
CHAPTER 17	The Precious Waste	111
THE FINAL WORD		117

CHAPTER 1

The Way of the Cross

You are most likely a serious Christian. At the very least, you are one who seeks a deeper understanding of "spiritual things." Otherwise, you probably would not have made the decision to read a book about the cross.

Even so, you may want to tighten up your seatbelt for the journey ahead. You see, dear Christian, there is a bit more to the message of the cross than you probably imagined. In fact, the very first thing you are about to discover is that there are actually two crosses. First and foremost, there is the cross of Calvary. That is, of course, the one on which Christ died for our redemption. It is by far the most famous cross in all of recorded history. Even so, it is not the only cross.

THE CROSS IN YOUR PATH

Just like most sincere believers, you have probably uttered words similar to the following: "I just want to be nearer to God." You have most likely sung a hymn or two along the line of "Nearer to Thee is all I want to be." No doubt, you really meant what you sang and prayed. Because you have officially enrolled your heart into discipleship training, you have also become a candidate for a deeper walk with the Lord. Spiritual thoughts are not easy to express. A spiritual mystery cannot be figured out even by the most intellectually superior among us. Spiritual things can only be revealed. The revealer is the Lord Jesus Christ Himself. It is important to Him that we see things from His perspective.

With that said, now may He reveal something of His mind as we attempt to put on paper some things which are not so easy to express. The cross in your path is one of those things. Remember that it is fundamentally different from the one on which Christ died. So this is where we begin, with the second cross.

The first cross was the Father's appointment for His Son. It was His alone to bear, and He finished the work of salvation there.

The second cross is the Son's appointment for you. This is the one that He asks you to take up. In fact, He commands that you deny yourself, take up your cross, and follow Him.

That first cross made the way for your spiritual birth, but the second cross is God's provision for your spiritual maturity. His cross was an event, but your cross is a process.

THE WAY OF THE CROSS

Every Christian has already received the benefit of that first cross. Every serious Christian will eventually encounter the second one, too. That is the inevitable one.

Yes, Christ died for us on His cross, and we died in Him. Now He asks us to die to our own self-centered life. His death was once for all; ours is to be daily. You have no doubt already figured out that this book is not going to be about the cross that made your conversion possible.

Yes, being born from above is the work of that redemptive cross. It is our beginning. The book you are about to read, however, is about the other cross—the one that transforms you. God's plan for you is that you should find yourself living on the high ground of spiritual thought and spiritual sensitivity.

The message of transformation might be politically incorrect. In fact, any message of self-denial has been mostly set aside for a more positive, upbeat, happy, nonchallenging one. Being in a typical church today is much like being "at home on the range where never is heard a discouraging word." Yes, many Christians actually consider any word having to do with transformation to be discouraging.

Apparently, if the Lord were passing through town today in human form, He would have to come up with a different message than the one which He spoke to the rich young ruler, because that message might hurt someone's feelings. He also would probably not be invited to speak at some of the seminars that have taken place in recent years.

THE CROSS IN YOUR PATH

There have been Christian seminars—not just seminars, but church-sponsored seminars—on everything from making profits in real estate to weight loss to raising successful children. Is becoming wealthy, skinny, and raising award-winning kids really the primary concern of the Lord's heart? Have you noticed that much of the New Testament has been replaced with a modern, professional, marketing strategy?

The truth of the cross, along with many of the Lord's commands, seems to have slipped right through our fingers and out of our spiritual consciousness. Spiritual thoughts do not volunteer to stay contained; they have a strong tendency to drain away. Perhaps they are not counted as precious, so we just allow them to drift away.

How different things would be if we realized that the cross really should be a normal part of our experience and not the exception. Neither is it something strange. It is God's perfect choice for our transformation. So, if you are ready, let us take a journey together and explore this inevitable cross.

WARNING:

You said that you would like to know the Lord better and have a deeper and lasting walk with Him. You claim to have an interest in the deeper things of the Christian life. Well, you are about to be tested. There is no such walk without the cross. There is no such life without a measure of suffering, and portions of that suffering will probably be with you for your entire life. As you grow older, you can expect the work of the cross to become deeper, more intense, and more demanding.

Why? Because God's plan is your brokenness. It is that you should become utterly and completely broken. The transforming work of the cross is His provision for the breaking of your natural strength and its roots. The crushing of that within you which demands its own rights will have to take place. We wish we could offer you a softer landing, but then you would hear the same old song rather than the true one. The progressive death of self-strength, self-confidence, and self-righteousness is the beginning of a deeper expression of His life in and through you.

So, welcome to the real Christian life.

CHAPTER 2

Rebekah

Love of the Gift Giver Versus Love of the Gifts

All believers will eventually find themselves at a crossroad. Actually, the crossroad will show up over and over in your spiritual journey, although it will never look the same on any two occasions. This is because the crossroad is simply nothing more than a place of decision. It is not the kind of decision where one can weigh the good options versus the bad ones. It is not the crossroad of logical decision, nor the place of calculated choice. You see, it is a place of spiritual decision, and all such decisions are matters of the heart rather than matters of the mind. Spiritual choices test your motives as well as your commitment.

THE CROSS IN YOUR PATH

> *"The refining pot is for silver and the furnace for gold, but the Lord tests hearts"*
>
> **~ PROVERBS 17:3**

One day you will look back over the course of your own life and perhaps be able to see how various choices at the designated intersections of life had everything to do with the final destination.

Please remember that we are not referring here to salvation. We are focusing on being prepared for brideship.

Perhaps Rebekah's story can help us to see.

Why is Rebekah's story pertinent to a book about transformation? It is because she is the type and picture of someone who became the bride for the Son. Her story is one of great encouragement to all who are being "made ready" in the midst of transformation, along with its tests and trials. You see, the transforming work can only be done in this life. Its outcome will only be revealed in the next life.

> *"And I saw the holy city, new Jerusalem, coming down out of heaven from God, prepared as a bride adorned for her husband"*
>
> **~ REVELATION 21:2**

Bible teachers often tend to be directed by attaching their focus to one particular truth at the expense of another one.

REBEKAH

The heroes and heroines of the Old Testament each represent one facet of God's multisided diamond. No one character contains the "whole story." It is by putting the lives of vessels such as Abraham, Isaac, Jacob, Joseph, Sarah, Rachel, and others together that spiritual principles become vision.

Rebekah is among those whom God has chosen to reveal one specific portion of His plan. Again, her story is not the entire one, but it is of primary and foundational value to every Christian who has set their heart toward a love relationship with the Lord.

The Scripture does not tell us in a specific way as to how Rebekah became prepared. It does reveal, however, that those who submit to the transforming work of the cross will receive both vision and relationship.

If you are still reading this, then you are probably already a believer, so you, dear reader, are already part of the spiritual family of Christ. It is only redeemed people who qualify for this testing that produces bride readiness.

Rebekah's story begins with one father's search for a bride. The bride will be for his son. The father here is Abraham, who assigns the oldest servant of his house to go and find that right girl.

Now, who do you suppose this servant pictures in the spiritual story? Abraham is the father, and his servant is a type of the Holy Spirit. After all, is not the Holy Spirit the servant in God's house today? It is the same Spirit who searches hearts today. He is always looking for those who will listen to His voice.

Abraham's servant loaded ten camels with fine gifts and set off on his journey. The servant arrived at the city well precisely at the time when women were coming out to draw water. His perfect sense of timing was no accident. The Spirit's timing is never random.

Our understanding of the spiritual is so limited; nevertheless, His time and choice of meeting places are always perfect.

Understanding is a well of life to him who has it. The choice of meeting at a well was also not a random setting. Wells are so often the very place where God chooses to meet. It was by a well in the wilderness that the Lord opened Hagar's eyes. It was at a well that Moses met his wife. It was at a well that our Lord Jesus asked a lost woman to give Him a drink of water. He asked first; then He revealed that it was He who could give her living water.

The servant prays that the girl to whom he chooses to speak might be the very one appointed to become the wife of his master's son. Why is it recorded in Genesis that the servant prayed for the perfect choice? Not only does the Spirit intercede for our heroine at the well, but He also intercedes for you, dear reader. Yes, He does intercede for us, but He also asks something of us. He intercedes and then asks a question.

The servant prays that the one to whom he requests a drink of water might also offer to water his camels as well.

REBEKAH

Precious gifts would follow later on for our sister, but not before she answers the Spirit's request. You see, He does not dangle the gifts at first. He is not Santa Claus.

When Rebekah appears at the well, she is "carrying her jar on her shoulder." This is not to imply that she had the shoulders of a linebacker. This refers to her spiritual strength. It is also mentioned that she was very beautiful and a virgin.

Of course, when asked, Rebekah offers a drink to the servant, and she volunteers to water the camels. By the way, thirsty camels consume a lot of water. Our sister knew this, and having already counted the cost, she nevertheless offered.

Then the servant posed another question: "Is there room for us to lodge in your father's house?"

Her answer: "There is plenty of room for you and plenty of straw and feed for the camels."

The point of this story is that when the master's servant came, Rebekah was heart and spirit ready to meet him. She was already prepared. She had been "made ready."

After she provided water for the ten camels, Abraham's servant gave her multiple gifts of precious golden jewelry. In Scripture, gold speaks of the divine nature.

The Spirit loves to give gifts, but the gift brings with it a potential for calamity. Are our eyes on the gift, or are they reserved for the Giver?

THE CROSS IN YOUR PATH

Rebekah ran home and told her family everything that had just happened. She showed them the golden gifts, and naturally, they were elated. So far, everyone is excited and caught up in the jubilation of this mysterious gift-bearing stranger.

At first, he is welcomed into the home of Rebekah's family. Then he begins to testify as to his purpose for this journey. He is seeking a bride for his master's son. The Holy Spirit in you is also seeking a bride for the Lord. For her part, Rebekah has already shown a disposition toward the Spirit in her willingness to serve the thirsty camels.

The dialogue between the servant and the family is beautifully presented. The servant retraces every single incident that took place since his first sight of our heroine at the well.

Rebekah did not brag or overstate anything that had happened. She had already demonstrated by her service that she possessed spiritual affection.

Those who love the Lord will discover that the Holy Spirit can tell their testimony with more insight than they ever could.

Remember that the family is caught up in the euphoria of the moment, but that moment does not last. Now the servant delivers the big reveal. He wants Rebekah to go with him to a distant land to become the wife of his master's son.

Wait just a minute! If you read the story, you will see that the family, who was open to the servant and who loved the gifts,

REBEKAH

now decides to attempt a negotiation. They just want Rebekah to stay home for a little while longer.

Most of us are a lot like Rebekah's family. We want our loved ones to have a relationship with the Lord. We want them to have spiritual gifts (boy, do we love those gifts!) and to have a testimony. We just have a problem with turning them over completely to the Holy Spirit. Can we not keep them just a little while longer and then a little more after that?

The servant said that he could not wait. We love the blessing, but do we love the Giver of good things?

Everyone involved agreed to consult Rebekah to allow her to make the final decision. When asked if she would go with this man, she gave her answer: "I will go."

Now, what about you? Will you go?

Perhaps there is already a well that is destined to become part of your personal story. Be encouraged in the knowledge that your Lord is quite capable of bringing you to that well and meeting you there. There is more than one well in the life of a Christian, just as there is more than one crossroad on the journey. When you find yourself at God's chosen crossroad (and you will), no one else can make the decision for you. Rebekah made the final decision.

There was some cost involved. She left her home and family to marry someone she did not know.

THE CROSS IN YOUR PATH

Does any of this sound familiar to you? Those who love the Lord are those willing to leave home, family, comfort, security, and everything else to follow Him.

Her story (at least this episode) is a picture of a wise young woman whose decisions led to her union with Isaac. The son received his bride. Yes, she was chosen, but she also made a choice. The very same God who worked in her heart through divinely orchestrated circumstances is the same One who has called you to deeper things.

CHAPTER 3

Job

---ᴖᴖᴖ---

The Christian life is a series of stages. In the previous chapter, we were able to witness a tender yet sovereign beginning to a love story. The deeper part of the story has to do with God's work in the heart. When you have eyes to see, you will begin to notice a similar theme over and over again in the men and women of the Old Testament.

We are not capable of expressing God's work in His holy ones with as much insight as we wish we could. Even so, let us continue to explore together something of God's intended work in the inner person.

We saw one stage in Rebekah. We will see another in Job.

Rebekah's story began when the Spirit found her at the well. Job's story began when God gave permission to the adversary.

THE CROSS IN YOUR PATH

Transformation is a procession of surrenders.

When difficulty, trials, or circumstances break into our lives, we tend to automatically assume that the cause must be (1) the bad people got in our way; (2) the devil is working overtime; or (3) God must be mad at me. Perhaps you are one of those Christians who believes that bad things happen to you because God is displeased with you, and therefore, you must be in sin. Well, here is a surprise: The Lord often allows and even engineers things in the lives of His chosen ones to help them arrive at a higher spiritual destination.

We ask the Lord to work in our hearts and to use us as He pleases, but are we shocked when He takes us up on our own prayer!

We prayed that prayer only because He put it in our heart in the first place and then gave us the grace to speak it back to Him. Perhaps our prayer to go higher and deeper found its way to heaven as a pleasing aroma to the Lord. So, what is His response to those who love Him? Get ready for a surprise!

Our scene opens in another realm. It is a day when angelic beings have gathered to present themselves before the Lord. Now, just envision that angels are there, along with archangels and all manner of wondrous beings. The place is the very presence of God Himself.

Upon closer inspection, we discover, to our astonishment, that even Satan himself is there. What is he doing in the throne room of the Most High? He certainly does not live there, for he has been cast out. His temporary home is in the skies surrounding earth, yet with access to earth. Well, it now appears that he also has visitation rights in the heavenlies as well.

Satan makes two appearances in heaven's court. He does not mention anyone's name. He seems to be minding his own business. Then comes an incredible and revealing scene. It is God who speaks first. He takes the initial action, not Satan.

"From where do you come, Satan?"

"From roaming about on the earth and walking around on it."

Watch now as God does something that most of us would have never seen coming. He brings up the name of someone as a potential choice for Satan. Amazing! Satan did not bring up any names. It was the Lord God who suggested a specific person to the adversary. Now, most of us would probably assume that if God is going to suggest someone by name to the enemy, then that person must be a sinful, wicked person who deserves punishment.

Let us take a brief pause and visit the earth. Somewhere on our little planet is a man who is simply minding his own business. He is not a wicked man. He is, in fact, guilty of nothing that would merit his being turned over to the devil. Even more flabbergasting to the conventional religious thought, the man in question is a servant of the Lord. His name is Job.

We are not at all sure that Satan knew every detail of Job's life. We are not sure that Satan was really all that aware of Job until God brought up his name. God made certain that both Job's name and his bio would be presented in detail to the enemy.

"Have you considered my servant Job? For there is none like him on the earth, a blameless and upright man, fearing God and turning away from evil."

Did you get that? Job is blameless and upright.

It sure blows a lot of modern theology, along with much of the most popular preaching of our day, to realize that it was God Himself who suggested that His servant Job should be the object of Satan's consideration. Think about that for a moment. Or, better yet, think about it for a year or two.

God, in an unseen realm that His servant Job cannot even imagine, introduces Job's name and lifestyle to the vilest, most unscrupulous, and heartless creature in the universe. If you have read the first couple of chapters of the Book of Job, then you already know that it was God who initiated all that was about to happen to Job. In the space of two brief conversations in heaven, the Lord gave Satan control over His servant's home, his wealth, and perhaps most devastating of all, his family. As if that was not enough, God also gave Satan power over Job's body with the only stipulation being that taking his life was off limits.

If you own a TV, a computer, a radio, or a smartphone, then you have, without a doubt, already been immersed in the following statements: "God wants you to rise to the top of your profession. God wants His people to be healthy, wealthy, and free of pressure. You should never get sick, much less suffer any serious affliction."

Apparently, the people who came up with this philosophy never read the story of Job. I guess they also missed these New Testament scriptures as well:

> *"Beloved, do not be surprised at the fiery ordeal among you, which comes upon you for your testing, as though something strange were happening to you"*
> **~1 PETER 4:12**

Or, Paul's words to the church at Philippi: *"For to you it has been granted for Christ's sake not only to believe in Him, but also to suffer on His behalf, experiencing the same conflict which you saw in me, and now hear to still be in me."*
~PHILIPPIANS 1:29-30

There seems to be a conflict here! In fact, the conflict is between the message from the Holy Spirit and that of some modern-day preachers.

As soon as Satan was able to gain God's permission, he went straight to work. Keep in mind that Satan had to first acquire God's permission. Satan wasted no time as he stirred up

THE CROSS IN YOUR PATH

raiders to steal Job's animals and kill his servants. Then fire fell from the sky and burned up Job's sheep, along with more of his servants. Then came another attack.

Things could not get any worse, right? Now comes a puff of cruel wind seemingly out of nowhere and brings about the death of Job's entire family. All of his precious sons and daughters are killed.

Mull this over in your mind for a moment: On top of the loss of his wealth, his security, and his family, Job was stricken with the affliction of a disease so horrible that it cannot even be fully comprehended.

If you sit down and read the entire story of Job, you will know that Job spent an agonizingly long season in disappointment, frustration, personal doubt, and confusion. Job's loss was a total loss. We know that his story had a happy ending; even so, the pain of loss and the accompanying memories of his loved ones surely left a deep wound in Job's heart; yet, he somehow remained steadfast.

> *"You have heard of the endurance of Job and have seen the outcome of the Lord's dealings, that the Lord is full of compassion and is merciful"*
> **~JAMES 5:11**

These words from James are inconceivable to the natural mind. How can a merciful God bring about such brutal calamity on one of His own dedicated servants? Does a loving Father really allow this kind of calamity to a spiritual child? Well, yes! It is not about what God should do, nor is it about what others ought to do. Again, your testimony is that which God has done for you and, even more importantly, *in* you.

Yes, it is true that Job's life story testifies to increase. We like that part. There is, however, a problem, for as soon as the pruning shears come out, we hide under the nearest bush. The work of pruning is always for the purpose of fruit-bearing. Wounding is for the purpose of spiritual increase.

Job's story is not one about getting his wealth back or ending up with better kids than before. Job's story testifies to the increase of union with God. It is a union that is costly and comes at the expense of other things via God's choosing.

There was no increase for Job until there was a complete and total surrender of all that the Lord desired. We know from the story's beginning that Job was a good person. We think that is enough. We are so deeply imprisoned by the concept of good and bad that we cannot see straight. Our preconceived ideas about how God does things and our embedded opinions on how things should be are all we need to keep us weak in sight and hearing.

Yes, Job was a good man, just not a complete one as to God's perfect plan. There was a course waiting for Job, and it is the same one that may be coming to you.

THE CROSS IN YOUR PATH

One big lesson that is waiting out there is the knowledge that God will alter our environment in order to speak to us. Even the Lord's servants can have slightly plugged-up ears. This was, in part, Job's issue.

He could not quite hear the Lord's voice, so the faithful Lord had to speak a bit louder. That louder voice usually comes through a change of circumstances. The challenge for us is not restoring the old environment; the real issue is hearing His voice.

Let us stop for a moment and look at the prophet Elijah. It was the same God who touched Job's world who also touched Elijah's. Job was a righteous man. Elijah was a faithful prophet. That he had seen and partaken of amazing events would be an understatement. He was a full-fledged, mighty prophet. Was that enough? No! God wanted more. (He always does!) So, the Lord engineered a perfect portion of discouragement for His servant and topped it off with a big, fat, ugly death threat from Queen Jez. Talk about distress!

So, our hero did the natural thing. He ran for his life and hid out in the wilderness. This scene pictures the loss of all self-confidence.

Have you noticed how much the Lord is interested in exposing and breaking self-confidence?

That is when an angel came to him with food and water. Then Elijah began to rest. Why do you suppose Elijah needed an angel to give him food? Those circumstances which led to pressure and the loss of all self-strength are the very things that allowed the angel of the Lord to provide nourishment.

Even gifted people (especially gifted people) must lose their self-strength, bravery, and especially the pride of past accomplishments. Elijah had to come to grips with his need for spiritual nourishment and learning to rest in the Spirit. In other words, he was learning of his need for total dependence on the Lord.

It sure would be nice if the Lord could just speak quietly to us and tell us that we need to surrender completely to Him. Who would argue? "Yes, Lord, I agree." It is too bad that it does not work this way. We do not disagree in principle; it is that we do not have the slightest idea as to what needs to be surrendered. We probably did not hear (or maybe would not listen) the thousand times He suggested our surrender of something specific.

So, He will most likely choose to blow on our lifestyle with its surroundings. We, just as those servants of the Lord before us, have no idea of the things in our hearts that are stopping up our ears and blurring our sight.

Past accomplishments and victories are not much good when it comes to facing down current circumstances, are they? Oh yes, we tend to lean so heavily on the memory of our past achievements. God, however, is not particularly impressed with us or our works. He is much more concerned with bringing us into the land of seeing and hearing. This land is reserved only

THE CROSS IN YOUR PATH

for small people. Most folks are too big to fit through the gate. This is precisely why our loving God must subtract before He can add. His breathing on our environment is a necessary provision for recognizing and surrendering those things that hinder our spiritual lives.

The self-life in us is usually much bigger than we realize. Even a small body can contain a giant self-life. We just cannot quite see it. In fact, you might even mistake this rascal's strength of will as spiritual power. Well, it is not! You might mistake your own rights as being the same as God's rights. Well, once again, God can defend His rights.

What He really wants is His right over you. Yes, He is committed to helping you to see the stronghold that has been constructed inside you.

Along the highway of life, many of us have developed a philosophy that keeps the Lord's voice at arm's length within the walls of our own personality. So, for us to actually hear the real voice of God, we first must face up to those notions that represent neither His voice nor His way.

We all have a history with the Lord. The problem is that we also have a history with ourselves. Now, a prophet needed to see the things that were not the voice of the Lord. Is it possible that you might have the same need?

It is very insightful to read Elijah's story and to consider what the Lord had to do so that His prophet could become truly

JOB

sensitive to His voice. The Lord showed Elijah a wind so strong that it could break rocks to pieces. Then the Lord showed him an earthquake. After that, He showed him a fire. Yet, the Lord was not in these things. Finally, after all this noise, our prophet could hear the sound of a gentle blowing. Then the Lord's voice came to him.[1] It was only then that Elijah could go and anoint others.

There will not be a true or deep anointing on your life until there is formed within you a submissive, dependent, quiet, listening soul. Or, do you think that you are better than God's prophet?

Every Christian contains at least some portion of the vision of Christ. Not every Christian, however, has a knowledge of their own self. We have such a strong tendency to determine God's voice through the filters of our own intellect, emotions, and intentions. You could probably also throw in some "life experiences" as interpreters.

The problem with this entire science is that it is nothing more than a study of the self as conducted by the self. You see, we must come to grips with those parts of our human makeup which imitate God's voice. Even though they masquerade with a lot of pomp and noise, they usually just drown out the real voice of the Spirit.

Elijah had to first see those elements that did not contain the Lord before he could hear the Lord's voice. It is not the Lord's

---

[1] You can meditate on these matters for yourself by reading. **1 KINGS 19.**

way to shout into your brain with a megaphone. He does not need to shout over your circumstances. His chosen way is by the gentle breathing of His Spirit into your quiet, listening spirit.

Now, let us return to Job. We have already seen that God's plan for His servant was one of spiritual union. We also saw that union with Him is costly and that it comes at the expense of other things.

It is often a challenge to accept the loss of those "other things" because they are not necessarily bad. They do not appear to present a problem to spiritual growth and, in many cases, they were given by the Lord in the first place. Please do not forget that our Lord is not obligated to answer the demands of our logic. The Lord does give, and the same Lord takes away. It is not because He is displeased; sometimes it is the very opposite. He is God, and we are not. Furthermore, the purpose of your life is not what you think it is.

Yes, the Lord restored abundant wealth to Job in the final scene of this story. He had fellowship with brothers and sisters, blessed with fourteen thousand sheep, six thousand camels, one thousand yoke of oxen, and a thousand female donkeys. According to my calculations, that is one fantastic retirement portfolio. As a super bonus, he had seven sons and three beautiful daughters.

These animals were all real, and the sons and daughters were real people. All of these served as tangible proof of God's faithful lovingkindness. Yet, the biggest gift was not in restoring things that Job had lost, for in the end he received something that he had never before possessed—spiritual sight.

Job's story is one of a man overcoming his own self-nature and becoming one who could actually bless the Lord. The journey may have begun at a point of self-righteousness, but it ended at the precious destination of deeper fellowship with the Lord. We do not realize just how important that fellowship is to our Lord.

Along the way, suffering becomes medicine, repentance becomes a bridge, and His faithfulness becomes food. Willingness to accept God's choices becomes essential.

CHAPTER 4

Paul

God's Grace Is Not Sufficient

Before you throw this chapter out the window, please give me a chance to explain. I was recently challenged by an old friend regarding the sufficiency of God's grace. He is a mature Christian, and just like you, I was initially shocked by his statement that God's grace is not sufficient.

Once the emotional dust had settled and some insight was offered, I began to understand his intended point.

God expressed personally to Paul that His grace was sufficient for him. Remember that this revelation came in the midst of a severe test when Paul was being afflicted by a messenger of Satan. First Job and now Paul. Who is next? Maybe you!

THE CROSS IN YOUR PATH

God did not say, "Do not worry; everything will turn out okay." He did not offer to remove Paul's affliction. He did not tell Paul to take a vacation or to seek professional counseling.

He simply expressed that His grace was sufficient for Paul. Now, most folks seem to assume that God said this as an automatic thing for all Christians. However, that is not exactly how the story goes.

The word of our Lord to Paul became Paul's personal possession. He proved this word as he walked it out in faith. (By the way, faith and grace are not the same thing. They are close relatives but not twins.)

You might expect that an apostle would have started his ministry with a Ph.D. from Heaven University with no need for further instruction. This is not how spiritual education works. Notice that I said spiritual education, not religious education. Righteous Job needed continuing education; so did Elijah. Paul got it throughout his entire life.

Indeed, Paul came to own the full sufficiency of God's grace.

How did he come to have this truth imprinted on his heart? He won a scholarship to the School of Christ. His own testimony is that he was beaten with thirty-nine lashes on five different occasions, beaten with rods three times, stoned once, was shipwrecked three times, and floated in the sea for a day and a night. He also crossed dangerous rivers and met robbers (2 Corinthians 11:24-26). Dangers on top of more dangers!

Paul's ministry included afflictions in multiplicity, along with being perplexed. Do not forget that along with all of this, he had a messenger of Satan to keep him humble.

> *"My grace is sufficient for you, for power is perfected in weakness"*
> **~2 CORINTHIANS 12:9**

There is a lot of noise these days about power and success, but the testimony of the apostles is one of personal transformation through divinely orchestrated suffering. God's own declaration for Paul and his future ministry was,

> *"He is a chosen instrument of Mine . . . I will show him how much he must suffer in behalf of My name"*
> **~ACTS 9:15-16**

Just to be perfectly clear, let us review the very first words that the Lord said about Paul. First, "He is a chosen vessel." Second, "I will show him how much he must suffer for My name's sake."

Job got it. Elijah got it. Paul got it. Even Christ learned obedience through the things He suffered. They all went through a course.

THE CROSS IN YOUR PATH

Now, what about you? Apparently, the real key to fruitful ministry is not by academic accomplishment, intellectual astuteness, marketing ability, or good looks. Personal transformation is God's plan. I know this will never sell, but it is still the truth.

Some colleges advertise that if you sign up for their classes, you will get personal attention from qualified instructors. Here is an even better deal: If you agree to education in the School of Christ, you will receive one-on-one personal attention from the Master Himself. If you choose to go the way of the cross, you will receive your very own "personalized course."

You might not get beaten with rods or be shipwrecked, but what you will get is the thing that you did not expect. You will learn that God is not interested in meeting your expectations. Thankfully, He is very committed to your transformation. After all, deep down in your heart of hearts, that is the very thing you most desire anyway. To please Him and to love Him are usually the very first markers on our spiritual journey. Then, sooner or later, we come to the realization that this life is not what we think it is.

It is a bittersweet revelation to discover that this life is not what we thought it was. It is a surprise, but thankfully, not a deal breaker. It intercepts our understanding of so many things that we take for granted.

Job had a wonderful family. Then it all changed in one gust of wind. While we want to know all of the wonderful and deep things that Job, Paul, and others came to possess, we just do not like the idea of how God chooses to work them into us. We want power; God wants weakness. We want at least some little bit of recognition; God wants humility.

"My grace is sufficient for you, for My power is perfected in weakness."

As I have already said, this was God's word to Paul. It was not necessarily spoken to you or to me that His grace is sufficient We know in our hearts that God does intend this to be for us as well. The trouble is that we are not absolutely sure just what the definition of grace is. I do not mean man's definition, but rather, the one that comes with understanding from above.

Some Greek scholars define grace as a divine influence upon the heart (Zodhiates) or as divine favor (Vine's). I like those definitions, but they are not exactly clinical absolutes, are they?

Faith is belief in that which God has spoken. It is not the result of positive thinking or even good intentions. It is not faith if you come up with an idea and then try as hard as you can to insist that God blesses your idea. You can only have faith in that which God has spoken either through His Word or by His Spirit. For faith to be exercised, you need to know the difference between yourself and the Spirit within you. The work of the cross will be a big factor in the discernment learning curve.

Another old friend of mine once told me that most Christians do not have a clue as to the right definition of grace. It is not a free pass regarding personal responsibility. It is the supernatural strength from God that enables you to love and obey Jesus Christ.

I know that my poor definitions are not very satisfying. That is because there is no absolutely perfect academic definition that I know of. Not to worry, though; there are clear and wonderful examples of both faith and grace revealed through the records of Scripture. We will take a more detailed look at this later, so stay tuned.

God's intention is that the same word revealed to Paul should also become your revelation. "How?" you ask. Paul's history with the Lord has been recorded by the Holy Spirit for both instruction and encouragement. You can read it and meditate on it.

Hopefully, you will gain some insight, but you still will not have Paul's experience. No amount of Bible study will give you that experience. Sorry, but you can only have Paul's experience by having Paul's experience.

"Now, wait just a minute!" is probably what you are thinking. "I do not really want trials or afflictions, and I certainly do not need a thorn in the flesh. I just want the revelation and power package."[2]

---

[2] Some Bible teachers love to ponder and speculate as to exactly what was Paul's thorn in the flesh. We do not know the answer because the Scripture gives us no real clue. However, we do know why he had it. It was to keep him from exalting himself.

Now, let us draw back the curtain for the big reveal. God desires to impart revelation. Great so far, right? However, revelation induces pride. Not so great! So, what can the Lord do in order for His servants (that is you, dear reader) to be able to receive spiritual insight and still remain isolated from stinky pride?

He just prescribes the perfectly measured amount of good old suffering. Not just any affliction will do, only the one designed specifically for you. Perhaps now is a good time to be reminded about the very first things that Jesus spoke regarding his servant: "He is a chosen instrument of Mine, for I will show him how much he must suffer for My name's sake."

By the way, many of the heroes of the Old Testament suffered with various forms of affliction, David in particular.

Spiritual affliction is not necessarily punishment. The affliction that comes from heaven is spiritual pressure for the sole purpose of causing its vessel to change course. When you see that heaven's definition is pressure for change, it brings you to the right understanding and the right definition. You can see Paul's change of direction from a life that was destructive and off-course to one of an intimate relationship with the Lord and fruitful service.

The one constant throughout Paul's life was suffering. He not only learned to accept it but also to see it as a kindness from the Lord.

THE CROSS IN YOUR PATH

> *"For our momentary, light affliction is producing for us an eternal weight of glory far beyond all comparison"*
>
> **~2 CORINTHIANS 4:17**

A less mature Christian would likely claim there is no such thing as momentary, light affliction. He would say that light affliction is an oxymoron at best.

It is only the mature one who is able to say, "Thank you, Lord, for helping me through this by grace and for the inward knowledge of an eternal weight of glory.

The closer you look, the more you will discover that there is no problem with God's grace or its sufficiency. The rub is that His grace probably does not mesh with your emotional sensitivities or intellectual requirements.

Oh, did I mention that His ways are higher than yours?

When trials and tests come our way, we usually feel ambushed and almost always surprised. Peter understood this, which is why he exhorted the holy ones not to be surprised at the fiery ordeals that would come for their testing, as if something strange was happening to them.

How often have you complained at the very first glimpse of a bump in your path? It is not an attack from Satan. Oh, we feel attacked all right. That is why we complain, gripe, murmur, curse, blame the devil, or blame our spouse, children, grandma, and the dog. Oh, I forgot to mention our leaders, pastors, elders, etc.

We are okay with Jesus having told Paul that His grace was enough for his affliction. We just have a little problem with accepting the other part: "My power is perfected in weakness." Is it possible that you may have been misinformed by your own preconceived notions? Did you confuse spiritual power with willpower, ambition, a glowing personality, and white teeth? I know that weakness is not what you ordered, but it is exactly what God prescribes for all who would become His fruit-bearing servants. Furthermore, He knows exactly what you need.

Once again, the real issue is not whether God's grace is sufficient for you. The real issue is simply that it does not always meet your expectations. The spiritual reality is that you need a measure of disappointment, heartbreak, and even trauma before you can appreciate and comprehend a bigger view of His ways.

This was the course that was good enough for Paul. Will it be good enough for you? May the sufficiency of His grace become your living testimony.

CHAPTER 5

Lazarus, Mary, and Martha

God's Grace Toward His Friends

Your Lord knows all that you need. He is kind. He cares for you. He actually cares about your joy and your peace, and yes, your growing up into spiritual maturity. Along the way, He will occasionally baffle you and leave you temporarily perplexed. He will not answer your most urgent questions or always make things clear to you. You see, He is God, and you are not. His ways are higher than your ways—not just better, but higher. His thoughts are higher.

There is perhaps no better description of how Jesus dealt with His own friends than the record of His interaction with Mary

THE CROSS IN YOUR PATH

and her sister Martha. Mary and Martha were true believers; furthermore, they loved Jesus.

They had a brother whose name was Lazarus. Now, surely our dear Lord would never allow any heartbreak to come to a true believer. Certainly, He would not allow disappointment to come to one who loved Him. Well, you should probably read John Chapter 11.

Jesus Christ, the creator of the universe, knew that His friend Lazarus was going to die. Yes, He knew, yet it seems that He did nothing to prevent it.

Here is the scene. Word of Lazarus' death comes to Jesus and His disciples. The disciples have absolutely no clue as to what is about to happen. When they hear the news that Lazarus has fallen asleep, they think that he is just taking a nap. So, Jesus cleared up the nap issue, but He still left the disciples a bit confused.

Jesus told them, "Lazarus is dead!" That is a pretty blunt statement but undoubtedly clear.

> *"And I am glad for your sakes that I was not there so that you may believe. But let's go to him"*
>
> **~ JOHN 11:15**

Thomas and the other disciples still did not understand what was happening. In fact, they totally misunderstood.

LAZARUS, MARY, AND MARTHA

Let us hit the pause button for a moment.

Hopefully, you are not thinking, "Those dumb disciples!" If you think that, you are probably just looking in a mirror. You see, we are disciples, and just like Tom and the boys, we have an incredibly strong tendency to lean to our own understanding. We like our understanding of things so much that we insist on it. In fact, we even insist that Jesus adjust Himself to our logic. He will not do that! He does not need to do that. He is God, and we are not. His ways are higher than ours, and His thoughts are higher than ours. That is where the work of the cross comes in. That work is a type of spiritual surgery that changes our view of things. It is a necessity.

Now, back to the story.

"If only you had been here." Those are the words that Mary and Martha both spoke to the Lord. They both said exactly the same thing. Interesting, is it not? Perhaps the reason for this is simply a reflection of the normal response …"if only." Whenever tragedy or trauma lands on us, we tend to immediately hit the logic button. There has to be some "if only" this or that had or had not happened. There must be a reason that will appease our logic. We reason as we search for more reasons. This is our way, but it is not the way of heaven. The Spirit is reasonable, but He is not the God of reason.

Our dear sisters had to discover a new and living way of relationship with the Master. They were not disbelievers, just

THE CROSS IN YOUR PATH

misunderstanders. They were just like us. Theirs was not a character problem. It was a "spiritual sight" issue. They simply needed a new way of responding to the issues of life.

How did they receive it? Their lesson is the same one that all disciples will wrestle with sooner or later. The Lord, in His perfect plan, will allow a crisis for you. It will not be just any crisis, either. It will be the perfectly orchestrated crisis with your name on it. In the midst of that crisis, He will not only test you, but He will also provide a perfect portion of the work of the cross. That portion will be God's surgical provision for your spiritual eyesight.

Unexplained suffering is always intended for God's ultimate good in you. It is His chosen way of spiritual advance.

Why?

It is not really necessary to place an order of importance to the various stages of the cross. This one, however, is excruciatingly painful, even though it does not necessarily involve physical pain.

The unanswered why can nearly melt a person's mind. Our sense of reason and our misplaced insistence on a logical conclusion can get gridlocked when the endless wheel of God's why is involved.

Have you ever passed through an event in life only to play it over and over again in your mind? Perhaps that one missing detail will pop up if we just play the scene one more time. The film keeps rolling in our minds, but there is no conclusion or satisfying arrival.

Our minds are like a hamster on his wheel. He runs and runs but never actually goes anywhere. This is us when we are stuck in the why.

So, you can pout, give in to hopelessness, or you could just go fishing. However, there is another choice: You can believe that your all-knowing and faithful Lord, who seems to be hiding Himself, will walk you through this season as He trains you to not live by your feelings, reasonings, or plans.

I once had a very, very close friend who was also a coworker. We were the best of friends for many years, and our wives even claimed that we were closer than brothers. My friend was a big man who was both physically fit and health conscious, yet one day he was diagnosed with a terminal disease. A few months later, he died.

My friend and I had traveled together in ministry around the United States and much of Europe. I had the opportunity to witness firsthand how his ministry touched the hearts of many people. He was also the primary teacher in our assembly. He died shortly before his sixtieth birthday, leaving behind a wife and five children, as well as a devastated community.

Why did our God allow this to happen? Why did God take him and leave me? I can only guess, speculate, and ask why.

THE CROSS IN YOUR PATH

What did this loss do to his dear wife and children, his mother, my wife, and all of those who loved and felt a bond with him? What about his ministry and all that could have been accomplished? Why did God take such a gift from the body of Christ and leave behind the less gifted?

You may ask, "Why will the Lord not answer me? I need an answer right now. Why did my brother, child, spouse, friend have to die? How can a loving God allow such a thing to happen?"

Dear reader, you are going to come face-to-face with your own unanswered questions at some point in your life. Sooner or later, you will find yourself dealing with an immutable God whom you do not understand. He is the same God whom Mary and Martha met. Those hours of unanswered questions and the thought of "if only you had been here" were all part of their perfect crisis.

We know that Jesus did, in fact, restore Lazarus back to life. Yes, Jesus can raise the dead, but He does not have to do that. He is not required to keep us from the sorrow of losing loved ones.

What He does promise is that He is the resurrection and the life. He did not restore Lazarus so that everyone in the story could live happily ever after. He raised Lazarus for the glory of God.

We are only capable of diagramming life's events from man's natural perspective. Christ, however, does not even attempt to explain Himself to the natural life. He goes straight to the spiritual other. That other is the other life, the other mind, and the other world. The Lord does not dumb down His language or His approach to problems. He does not seem the slightest bit interested in keeping us in childcare.

We ask natural questions; He gives us answers that do not make sense to the natural human way of thinking. The sooner we decide to come under the Lord's way, the sooner we leave the path of confusion.

Please remember that the Lord's ultimate plan is to bring you into a place of nearness—nearness to His thoughts, His plans, and His ways. The way of the cross is God's way.

The way of the cross is almost never one you had planned. That is partly due to its purpose, which is to deliver you step by step from your thought pattern to His.

Now, a question for your consideration: Do you suppose that Lazarus was ever the same again after having walked out of that tomb and having his death cloth unwrapped? What about his sisters? Do you think they were ever the same after having been eyewitnesses to life restored? You can be sure that neither he who came out of that tomb nor those who witnessed the scene were ever the same people again. They still had their personalities and human side, but their vision of divine life was forever changed. Eternal life became more than a theory on that day.

THE CROSS IN YOUR PATH

Eventually, the warranty on their bodies would run out: Mary, Martha, and Lazarus all died. How or when we are not told, because that is not the point of their spiritual history. Their spiritual history is not the history of super Christians. They were just regular folks who loved Jesus. They were much like you and me in that we love Him, even though we do not always understand Him. They were not super-spiritually mature or overcoming giants of faith, either. Again, they were a lot like us.

Neither they nor you and I were ever expected to make ourselves into mature, spiritually-minded Christians. In fact, we cannot do that, but God has made His own provision for us. Great news, right? Well, it is the same provision that He made for His own Son. He learned obedience by the things He suffered.

I am sorry to deliver such hard news, but divinely orchestrated suffering, along with its companion disappointment, is a major part of God's provision. You do not usually understand it (see Job); you do not like it (see Paul); you are often confused by it (see Mary and Martha). On top of all that, you would probably get out from under it if you could (see self in the mirror).

The heart of their stories, as with all true disciples, is one of divinely chosen events. Circumstances that bring seasons of doubt, seasons of "if only," and seasons of real loss are all part of God's perfect agenda for His loved ones. All disciples have a personal part in the story of the cross, and the cross also has a part in their story.

LAZARUS, MARY, AND MARTHA

What will the work of the cross reveal in your life? What will the heavenly record show? It is that interior work through outward circumstances which is the necessary requirement for all who would become nearer to Christ. Your transformation is God's idea and thus includes His perfect plan for its accomplishment.

None of us knew Mary, Martha, or Lazarus, so it is easy to gloss over their story without noticing the agony of death. It is even easier to dismiss Job's children as being merely characters in a story and forget that they were real people. Job came to the right end through all of this. It is not so difficult to accept Bible characters as having found grace and faith in the midst of fiery trials, but it is a little different when the reality of loss personally comes to us.

You probably know someone who has endured the loss of a child. I have known several families in my lifetime who have suffered the death of a newborn baby. I have friends who have lost a teenager. My wife and I have had our own experience of this.

The devastation of such an event is about as horrific as anything could be; yet, as terrible as it is, the loss can be only the beginning of pain. The trauma and hurt often lead to another form of agony—the unanswered question: "How could God allow this?" One of the larger aspects of spiritual anguish is the silence that meets this question. We want an answer. Our minds need one, while our emotions demand one. (Perhaps our question was not really a question as much as a complaint.) Either way, heaven remains silent. It feels as though our Lord has become coldly absent.

I confess that it was not so difficult for me to believe for Job or Mary and Martha, but it was another matter altogether when I became part of the story. How is this terrible event supposed to help me believe? How? That is the initial chorus of our mind and emotions. How can I trust a God who allows a thing like this to happen? (Maybe there was a trust problem from the get-go.)

Thankfully, we have a God who is patient, loving, and understanding of everything that has befallen us. This Lord who loves you and knows all about you is the same One who longs for you to know Him and to know His ways. He only reveals His deeper heart to those who love Him, and because you love Him, He has determined to share a portion of His very own why. We may never know the fullness of Christ's why in His hour of being forsaken; yet, we have been chosen for our own hour.

> *David knew. "I know, Lord, that Your judgments are righteous and that You have afflicted me in faithfulness"*
>
> **~ PSALM 119:75**

His judgments are perfect and perfectly timed. His intent is always for our perfecting. Our Lord knows every single thing that will come into our lives. He knows what He has appointed, as well as that which He will allow. The good news is that He never, ever asks us to do anything that He has not already given us the grace to do. So, please do not get discouraged when you realize that those things do not come automatically. They did not come automatically for Mary or Martha, either. Even our promise to never leave Him will eventually fail. Most honest folks over the age of twenty-five will admit that it has already failed. It is not our commitment that wins the day; it is His commitment to us to bring us into a greater fullness of spiritual life upon which our hope should rest. That is, in fact, why He saved us. It is not for salvation to be an end in itself, but so that He can raise us up into the full measure of spiritual maturity.

The maturing life is a process that begins with a surrender to the cross and ends in brokenness. Answers do not come at the beginning; they come as we pass through the various appointed trials of life. The seemingly unanswered why only finds its conclusion when we are able to see the fruit of brokenness. When we can acknowledge that being crushed is the only way that leads to our release from the bondage of self-righteousness, then we begin to both see and even appreciate the why. He is reminding you and teaching you that you can now deny yourself, take up your cross, and follow Him.

CHAPTER 6

The Ark

How fascinating it must have been for the Hebrew children to watch the Tabernacle being erected! Our scene opens early one morning. The previous day, a site was chosen and carefully prepared. First, the site had to be cleared and leveled. All around were priests carrying various portions of the Tabernacle. Each man waited his turn to get his part in the proper place.

As the poles and various materials were assembled, it was of absolute importance that each and every piece was placed exactly according to God's previous instructions. The pattern that God had revealed to Moses left nothing to man's ingenuity or imagination. This tabernacle in the wilderness of Sinai was to be a testimony of God's covenant with His people.

THE CROSS IN YOUR PATH

At the center of this amazing tent, the priests would place the Ark. The Ark is the center; everything else rests on it or around it. What does this Ark represent, and why is it at the center?

The Ark is Christ. He is the center, and all else is measured by and finds its proper place in relationship to Him. The center of God's plan is more than Bible study, prayer meetings, or even Christian service. The center of everything is the Lord Jesus Christ Himself.

The tabernacle which Moses built had a section called the Holy Place. Behind that was a second veil and a sacred tent known as the Holy of Holies. Only the high priest could enter that place, and even then, only once a year. Before going in, however, he had to offer a blood sacrifice. This sacrifice was the only way for the priest to get released from his own sins, as well as those of the people. But when Christ appeared as a high priest of the good things to come, He entered through the greater and more perfect tabernacle, the one not made with human hands, that is to say, not of this creation.

The blood of Christ, the ultimate sacrifice, has made the way for us to enter the Holy of Holies. You and I can now have spirit-to-Spirit fellowship with the Living God because of Jesus Christ, our personal high priest. Our redemption was made possible because He became the blood sacrifice for us.

I suppose that most folks who are still reading this book already knew the things written so far in this chapter. Those

THE ARK

things needed to be said even though they are elementary to most Christians. They needed to be stated because of what is about to be said.

Remember that the purpose of this book has to do with the cross of transformation rather than the cross of salvation. There can be no transformation without salvation first. Furthermore, there needs to be a clear sense of salvation in order to keep us from a sloppy, guilt-ridden, self-propelled kind of transformation.

Remember, the Ark became seemingly hidden somewhere in the depths of the Tabernacle. That young boy who witnessed the Tabernacle being erected had a growing desire to get inside in order to reach that Ark. Once erected, the Tabernacle had a cloud hovering about it. It was not just a cloud but *the* cloud. When that cloud moved, it was time for the people to break down the tent and move. Then the entire thing would be reassembled, and once again, the Ark was always in the center.

Every Hebrew heart desired to be there with that Ark. We want to be there, too. So, as we approach the entrance, we are fixed on the holiest place of all. It is a straight shot from the entrance right on through to the spot where the Ark rests. We are enchanted with the idea of seeing it, touching it, and just being in its presence. We are almost there, at least in our desire.

Then, there suddenly comes a very rude awakening. There is a jarring sight as you pass through the front entrance. Right smack dab in your path is this thing that is blocking your way.

THE CROSS IN YOUR PATH

Oh, it is an altar. You cannot go on into the deepest part of the Tabernacle nor to the riches that are hidden there.

Okay, let us pause for a moment. You thought we had already declared that the entrance was secured by Christ's sacrifice. That is right; salvation is accomplished. Deepest fellowship, however, is still pending. You see, that requires a different sacrifice.

There is no other sacrifice for salvation. Christ died once for all. The sacrifice for which He asks is so that you, as a child of grace, can grow into mature, deep, heart-bonding marriage material. He is seeking a bride, and she is being prepared to be just that. Remember Rebekah, the example of spiritual preparation.

Okay, what is the sacrifice for which Jesus Christ asks? It is not a dove, a bullock, or a sheep. The sacrifice is you—your very life! There is a declaration from the New Testament that has been passed down over the centuries and is now calling out to us.

> *"Therefore I urge you, brothers and sisters, by the mercies of God . . ."*
> ~**ROMANS 12:1**

There is a record of mercies, graces, and gifts throughout the Scripture, but after these things are experienced, there comes a call. We love those graces. When we are first saved, we are fascinated with the idea of spiritual gifts. We are captivated by the possibilities, and those things helped draw us to Christ. Then came the first tones of a gentle call.

THE ARK

Because of the modern world's loss of spiritual vocabulary, the words may seem peculiar, but the message is as clear as ever: "Therefore I urge you, brethren, by the mercies of God, to present yourselves..." It is not a bull that He wants, nor a lamb. It is especially not an excuse. What He wants is you!

It would be nice if the call ended right there. (It does not. I think you already know the next line.)

"Therefore I urge you, brothers and sisters, by the mercies of God, to present your bodies a living and holy sacrifice, acceptable to God, which is your spiritual service of worship."

Those three words—a living sacrifice—change everything! In a spiritual sense, we are never really intended to get past that altar. It is a beautiful and wonderfully mysterious matter that Christ desires deepest union with us and yet requires us to live at the altar. "Take up your cross daily."

Oh, how we need the faithful voice of the Holy Spirit to continually draw our hearts back to the altar. It is not for condemnation; there is absolutely no spiritual value in beating ourselves up or indulging in any form of religious penance. The altar is a place where you and I can offer a sacrifice that is a sweet-smelling aroma unto heaven.

There is, however, a specific thing that needs to be put on the altar. In fact, it needs to be offered up again and again. The thing that must be offered as a continual sacrifice is none other than the heart—a heart that is willing to suffer the loss of anything and everything that stands in the way of its own union with Christ. This is the most pleasing sacrifice.

A heart on the altar is one that says: "All my ambitions, all my plans, all my hopes and dreams, all that I am, and all that I have, I surrender to my Lord." Anything that stands between you and the union that Christ desires with you must be willing to die. That spirit of willingness is the sweetest aroma that you will ever offer up to heaven. You could become a missionary to Siberia, start an orphanage in Guatemala, or sell your surfboard and give the money to the poor, but none of this will necessarily bring joy to our Lord.

It is not the thing that you decide to do or the thing that you want to do. It is not giving in to a romantic, religious calling to serve the poor of Swahililand. That is probably just a result of a wonderful story that you read once upon a time about someone else's calling, someone else's sacrifice. The only sacrifice that you are asked to make is to give your heart on the altar.

I know it is scary, but the encouraging thing is that we have a God whose judgments are perfect. Our problem is that we would much rather pick and choose as to what is going to die on that altar. That is because we either do not really trust the Lord or are unwilling to give up some things. When you do place yourself on the altar with all of self's ambitions, plans, and hopes, you are turning them over to the One who judges perfectly. We are lousy, slippery, imperfect judges, especially when it comes to qualifying our own wants and supposed needs. Our Lord, however, knows exactly what needs to die and when! It is a trustworthy God who resides in the Holy Place.

After the Smoke Clears

For some, Christianity begins and ends with only the initial salvation experience. For some folks, that is the whole story—beginning, middle, and end. Their practice of Christianity is nothing more than a variation of religious reproduction. It is not much of an overstatement to suggest that their definition of the "crucified life" is that since Christ died for our sins, there is nothing else to do. It is an absolute truth that Christ died for our sins, but it is also true that He now asks something of us. He asks us to deny ourselves.

Take up your cross.
Come follow Me.
Deny – take up – follow.
Daily.

CHAPTER 7

Entitlement

Dear reader, one of the greatest mistakes a believer can make is treating an episode of transformation as one and done. It is possible to truly and experientially meet the cross with all of its dimensions and yet fall into the misconception that your encounter was enough. After all, it was a vivid, overwhelming, and life-changing encounter. Surely it was enough, right?

Nope! As wonderful and important as it was, it was still just one part of the journey.

Transformation is not an event; it is a process. That initial experience can become blurred with time. Then you will one day turn a corner, and once again, there stands a cross! You probably will not recognize it as what it really is. Instead, you might only see unfairness, betrayal, or mistreatment. In that unguarded moment, the very person who once knew the cross now rebels against it.

You probably will not see yourself as being in rebellion. In fact, you will most likely feel certain that as an older and wiser Christian, you are doing the proper thing, especially under the circumstances. It is only later, and then by the grace of God, that you realize you missed an opportunity to die to your self-life. Oh, you did allow the cross to work in some areas of your life, but you missed the vital area of God's present concern.

There are a few common problems that befall us as we get older. Our joints get stiff, our hearing diminishes, and our eyesight is not quite as sharp, but the common spiritual problem is that we think we no longer require the Lord's dealings. Having come through that initial season of testing brought great joy and a sense of satisfaction. However, it may have also ushered in a sense of entitlement.

The Lord never really stops the divine work of reduction. Do you remember how He kept reducing the size of Gideon's army until it was suitable for His purpose? He did not need a bigger army in order to gain victory over His enemies. The Lord eventually comes to that which seems to be both a good idea and a legitimate one. That which appears to be a good idea to us is often a hindrance to God's plan. He does not need our good ideas, just our obedience. Yes, the cross will eventually come for all good ideas.

ENTITLEMENT

When the cross comes, it is not your sin or your weak spots that the Lord is after. It is the heart that He seeks. We all agree that the Lord should have full possession of our hearts. The problem is that we do not know some of the things that are lurking in there. Because we cannot see all that is there, it is difficult, if not impossible, for us to recognize Him when His cross comes for one of those hidden things.

It would be easy to agree with the Lord if He came for anything that we knew to be wicked, evil, or immoral. It is a completely different matter, however, when He comes for our attachments. This issue gets even fuzzier because some of our dearest attachments came from Him in the first place. Or, did they?

If you are old enough to have grandchildren, then this is for you. Our families are a gift from God, and there is some scriptural justification for this. Children and grandchildren are not the problem. The place that is given to them in our hearts is the problem. It is not natural to suspect that your affection for loved ones could ever crowd in on the ground that God has reserved for Himself. In fact, you probably do not even think it could be a possibility.

The real problem is that we do not know our own hearts. The thing that the Lord is after is what we least expect.

He is not always after bad things. Those are usually not so difficult. It is the good things that lodge themselves in our

THE CROSS IN YOUR PATH

secret hearts and will not let go. It is the unexpected and unknown to us that He seeks.

> *"Little children, guard yourselves from idols"*
> ~ 1 JOHN 5:21

He wants your heart with all of its hopes and dreams, affections, and yes, attachments.

> *"The one who loves father or mother more than Me is not worthy of Me"*
> ~ MATTHEW 10:37

By the time we are old enough to have grandkids, we have probably already had a lot of life experiences. That is okay, but it is not okay if we settle down spiritually and say to ourselves (subconsciously, of course) that we have gone pretty far with the Lord and paid enough dues. Now, it is time for me to reward myself and just relax with my _____. That line was left blank so that it can be filled in with hobbies, TV, travel, family, affections, or attachments.

The sense of entitlement is an enemy who would love to sneak into the camp of your heart. You probably will not recognize such an enemy because it comes disguised as something good. That sense of entitlement never confesses that his good is intended to intercept the best or that he is, in fact, an enemy. He just hopes that you will not recognize the transforming

ENTITLEMENT

work of the cross when it comes to exposing him and ultimately causing his expulsion from your heart.

When you read 1 and 2 Kings, one of the things that jumps off the pages is how various kings started their reigns with anointing and even spiritual vision, only to wander off and end badly. Some started with wonderful achievements but eventually failed due to a lack of self-knowledge. Some strayed from trusting God to self-preservation. Some fell victim to pride, others to lust for power, some to jealousy. At least one started like a spiritual racehorse, only to settle down into the comfort of past achievements.

The cares of life did not evaporate, not even for kings and prophets. Your recognition of your need for the continuous work of the cross in your life is the only real safety net. It is a safety net especially for times of failure. That is why we must return to the altar whenever we find ourselves lulled to sleep by a past experience. Any past experience, no matter how valid, can never take the place of a current living sacrifice.

Dear one, complacency is an enemy. Entitlement is poison.

There is no such thing as a once-for-all experience of the cross. We need the Lord's continuous work in us until that day. Do not live in the past, whether it seems to be good or bad. Not only is the work of the cross inevitable for you and me, but it will inevitably return.

CHAPTER 8

Consecration

Certain theologies take a position that seems to think of transformation as a contradiction to salvation. That position tends to see any aspect of transformation as a counter to "saved by grace."

> *"But a natural person does not accept the things of the Spirit of God, for they are foolishness to him; and he cannot understand them, because they are spiritually discerned"*
>
> ~1 CORINTHIANS 2:14

The natural man referred to above is not an unsaved man; he is just an unspiritual one. Plenty of saved people are not yet spiritual, much less spiritually-minded. When, out of love the Spirit pricks your heart with the realization of your lack of

THE CROSS IN YOUR PATH

spiritual-mindedness, it is not a sign that you need to get saved again. It is not the devil's condemnation, either. It is the gentle voice of your Lord wooing you to give that unfinished part of yourself over to Him.

New birth is an event. Transformation is a process. A step in that process is often labeled as consecration.

Consecration always gets tested. Consecration in youth gets tested, as well as consecration in adulthood; however, the tests come in different forms and with different consequences.

I know a man who, as a youngster, made a vow to the Lord every summer at church camp for about ten years in a row. Every summer on the last night of camp, with the fire burning low and the campers all singing choruses, he, along with others, made vows to follow Jesus with a whole heart. No turning back!

Well, in a good year, that vow would last up to an entire two weeks—one week before school started and one week after. The young man was not insincere when he made his vow; he just did not know that he was a victim of his emotions and that those emotions, along with his own immaturity, set him up for failure.

Emotions make a good friend but a terrible leader. Of course, the whole campfire and song thing made the perfect stage for falling in love with the idea of consecration.

I know this young guy very well; I was that young man. He is not young anymore. I guess I was a bit embarrassed as a boy when my great vows got tested.

CONSECRATION

Perhaps I am not alone. It is amazing how consecration (no matter how well-intended) gets tested. It is always a surprise to discover the areas of life in which the Lord chooses to work.

In fact, surprise is a word that the work of the cross exemplifies. His cross is never what you think it is. He never comes for the thing that you expect, nor does He come in the way that you expected. You may find yourself surprised by your own reaction.

Perhaps the biggest distraction of the cross in adulthood is that we simply misjudge it. Our sympathy for our poor, misunderstood, and unfairly treated self tends to distort things. "This cannot be the cross. It must be a mistake. This is not fair!" Oh yes, there is always the devil to blame.

Because of the Lord's kindness and patience, He will often breathe a puff of clarity into our otherwise confused minds. In that moment, we see with clarity that the real issue is not our friends, nor our enemies, who are responsible. It is not the devil, either. The real problem is that big fat mistake we made when we consecrated our life to the Lord. Do you remember when you said to the Lord that He could work in your life in any way and by any means that seemed right to Him? Do you remember when you said that you really did want to be changed by the power of His life and by the cross? Now you are surprised to discover that He really heard your prayer and decided to take you up on it.

THE CROSS IN YOUR PATH

Sometimes we are tempted to ask for a start-over. "Lord, I guess I did not really mean all that I said. It was late, I was tired, and, come to think of it, I had skipped a healthy breakfast. Could you please just release me from my vow?"

The answer is no! You can beg, holler, scream, make demands, and throw dust in the air if you want. You consecrated your life to God, and He took it seriously. Thankfully, He is reluctant and possibly unwilling to let us escape from our vow. He heard you when you said that you wanted to give yourself for His service. He also heard you when you invited Him to have His total way in your life. He heard, and He said yes.

It is only later that we begin to discover that this life is not what we thought it was, and the cross turns out to be less romantic and more penetrating than we ever bargained for. You gave Him your life, and in return, you got a lot more than you had planned. Now you have to be encouraged by reminders again and again.

This is not the devil, circumstances, bad people, the angry judgment of God, or bad luck. (There is no such thing as luck for a Christian—good or bad.) It is the transforming work of the cross, and behind that cross is a still, small voice declaring that He is making you ready for a spiritual future.

CHAPTER 9
Success and Failure

We live in a world where the word success is the byword in Christian marketing. Once upon a time, the pope collected boatloads of money from the sale of indulgences. That was the marketing strategy from a few centuries ago. Just sell people trinkets to help get their relatives out of purgatory.

Today's scheme is not so much about selling trinkets, though some evangelists still do. The big sell today is the sale of a concept: Buy our books, listen to our podcasts, and attend our seminars. You can have it all. You can have power, wealth, great health, happy days, star-filled nights and, most of all, success in all you do.

Whoever came up with this idea was a genius. It sells big time!

THE CROSS IN YOUR PATH

Have you ever wondered why Jesus did not try this approach? Just think what He could have accomplished if He had just come down from the cross in front of a multitude of astonished onlookers. Jesus took a course that seems to be in direct contrast to the slickly-produced theatrics of modern Christianity. Did He not realize that in submitting to His Father's will, He was ruining an otherwise spectacular opportunity?

Furthermore, how much good was actually accomplished by His resurrection from the grave with no media coverage? If this sounds like a recipe for market failure, welcome to the real message of the cross. Jesus willingly chose the appearance of loss and weakness over one of power and victory.

Paul chose to boast only about his personal weakness. I guess he should have kept quiet about his multiple beatings, lashings, shipwrecks, etc. He could have had a lot more popular ministry if he had only spoken about success. The greatness of revelations received was okay, but he should have left out the part about his "thorn in the flesh."

You have probably gotten the point by now. Those who really know the work of the cross on a personal level know that failure and defeat are part of that work. Of course, you already know that had Jesus Christ vanished from the cross, the only one who would have won a victory would have been the devil. Of course, this is in the context of salvation. No death

SUCCESS AND FAILURE

on the cross would mean no salvation for us. But the Lord's seeming defeat upon the cross actually goes deeper than salvation. That seeming defeat brought about the defeat of all powers that have ever arrayed themselves against Him.

Still, it is difficult not to succumb to the popular message. It is nearly impossible to even address its errors due to its popularity. Does not a gigantic church building with talented praise leaders, a mega sound system, comfy seats, and a charismatic leader make for a great testimony to the world? Is it not a super idea that you could have everything the world has to offer and Jesus, too?

Upon closer review, a new discovery comes into focus. This discovery is not really new at all. It is the realization that the concept of defeat is part of God's nature. The themes that Jesus Christ referred to frequently in His teachings were the ones concerning surrender and loss.

> *"For whoever wants to save his life will lose it; but whoever loses his life (self-life) for My sake will find it"*
>
> **(MATTHEW 16:25).**

> *"If anyone wants to come after Me, he must deny himself, take up his cross daily, and follow Me"*
>
> **(LUKE 9:23).**

THE CROSS IN YOUR PATH

> *"For whoever wants to save his life will lose it, but whoever loses his life for My sake, this is the one who will save it"*
>
> **(LUKE 9:24).**

> *"The one who is least among all of you, this is the one who is great"*
>
> **(LUKE 9:48).**

While we Christians proclaim and exalt success, our Lord proclaims something quite different.

Here is a story that has been played out an infinite number of times. The circumstances may vary, but the basic point of the story is the same—defeat.

Someone is standing before a board. It might be deacons; it could be the church elders; it may be business associates. The common theme is that they are unhappy with him and want to throw him out.

The object of contempt is not a spiritual giant. He is not full of strength. He is, in fact, a normal guy with all the human weaknesses and fears of mankind. He would love nothing more than to find the door of escape from the pressure of this moment. He is concerned about his own future well-being and even more so about the economic survival of his family.

SUCCESS AND FAILURE

Yet, as we look closer, we do not see anger. We do not see hostility. What we see is a man who says, "Okay, gentlemen, have your way."

It will only take about twenty-four hours until word of his removal has gone viral. Certain things are sure to be repeated over and over again: "Have you heard about so and so? What a loss! What a shame! What an embarrassment!"

Yes, it all smacks of loss and personal defeat, at least on the surface, but something deeper is happening. First, the circumstances that created the perfect storm for this man were all allowed by the Lord. Secondly, deep down in the well of his spirit, he sensed the Lord's presence (though not peace) even in the midst of this trial. Lastly and most important of all, the Lord had a plan all along.

The man in our story had just enough grace to accept and allow a crushing experience to come into his life. His loss was real and brought real hurt, but there was also the possibility of something to be gained that could never be lost.

You see, in being crushed, defeated, and humiliated, it became a real possibility that this man would never again suffer temptation in the areas of security and finances.

Cowardice regarding the fear of men has lost its power. It might just be that in the season of devastating personal defeat, a giant step was taken in God's chosen direction.

THE CROSS IN YOUR PATH

> *"A man is no fool who gives what he cannot keep in order to gain what he cannot lose"*
>
> ~ JIM ELLIOTT

David is not remembered for his great strengths as much as for his brokenness. Again, we recall Paul's own words:

> *"For when I am weak, then I am strong"*
>
> ~ 2 CORINTHIANS 12:10

Had Christ stepped down from His cross, an incredible paradox would have taken place. In that moment, Satan would have won; yet, in Christ's humiliation and death, He was victorious, and Satan was defeated.

Now, will the Holy Spirit be able to reach the innermost part of your being and speak to you: "If you will lose now, you will gain later." Are you willing to stand against your natural instincts? If so, that moment of surrender and defeat will have turned into victory. If your heart is clean and your motives are clear, and if all of this is truly done before God, then suffering will be turned to victory.

When you read the writings of spiritual Christians and listen to the words of those who have been through the fire, you will encounter the message of surrender. In bitter tears, they surrendered even to the worst possible things that could happen to them, and out of this, God gave life.

SUCCESS AND FAILURE

Who among us has not faced a thought or a circumstance so horrible to our mind that caused us to beg, plead, and bargain with God not to have this required of us? Yet, when the spirit of repentance and the heart of agreement say yes to the Lord, there is a giant breakthrough. The spiritual roadblock in our path begins to dissolve.

Compare that end with the one that comes from pulling yourself free from the cross. You would escape the pain, but only to have it replaced by all sorts of self-justification.

May we all finally give up on self-preservation, turn, and move on up the slopes of Calvary.

CHAPTER 10
Decentralization

Who is on the throne? This is an easy question to ask but perhaps not so easy to answer, especially if one is being honest. Why? Because something within us resents Christ's claims in our lives. There comes a day when we find ourselves moaning and groaning over some of the issues in our lives.

There is a demand in us that says, "I have a right to my own life" or "I have a right to myself." Back in that season of initial consecration, we gave the Lord consent over our lives. We gave Him absolute authority over every natural inclination, every secret room in our heart, and even our gifts. We gave Him our ambitions, our hopes, and all of our plans.

That consecration embraces the past, the present, and the future. By now, you must know that it was never intended to

THE CROSS IN YOUR PATH

be one and done. It seems there is always something a little deeper that the Lord would like to dig out of us. Do not expect Him to stop digging.

The Lord never said that we should just take up our cross for a few years, and that would be enough. He said, "Take it up daily." Expect the work of the cross to remain active for the rest of your days on this earth. By the way, when you deny yourself, something dies.

The Christian life is a continuous experience of dying to self. Things we lose do leave an empty place, but that empty place gets filled with Christ Himself. You lose; you gain Christ. What a wonderful tradeoff!

The Holy Spirit keeps continually asking the same question: Who is on the throne of your heart—Jesus Christ or you? Many things come up when we realize that we are still occupying part of the throne. Maybe I should just try harder to be a good Christian. No, that is not it!

Actually, the only thing that you need to do is to submit. That's right; just submit. Submit to what, exactly, you ask. Well, the Lord is committed to helping us in this matter, and He is fully capable of arranging divinely-orchestrated circumstances just for you. Those circumstances never announce that they are manufactured by God. They just appear as random problems, distractions, and so-called bad luck. The more severe ones show up as health scares, financial

DECENTRALIZATION

problems, and the always dependable relationship issues. All of these circumstances are known and allowed by a loving and all-knowing God. Why?

When you look back over your own history, you will see that your greatest growth did not come in the seasons of greatest blessing. Your growth came in times of deep dealings with God. It came out of seasons of unanswered questions and even emptiness.

The Lord loves to bless His people. After all, one of His traits is "a loving Father who knows how to give good gifts to His children." The problem is that those seasons of blessing tend to make us feel special. We become independent and start believing that God must be very pleased with us.

Stand by; your Lord is coming with a divinely-created circumstance that has your name on it. Its intention is to tear down that little house of straw and replace it with something eternal. Some form of affliction is in the path of every child of God who is destined for transformation. Do not get too upset. Please remember that spiritual affliction is simply a perfectly chosen form of pressure that is intended to cause a change of course. That pressure is God's perfect way of keeping you and me on course.

Being on course is really what we all want. We just cannot do it by ourselves, and thank God, we do not have to do it on our own.

THE CROSS IN YOUR PATH

Here is one more angle on our theme. All the various stages of the cross are intended for the decentralization of your own life and toward the centrality of Christ in your life. Perhaps there is no greater contradiction to the natural mind than the words "to die is gain." The very law of eternal life is written in those words. The allowing of God's choices brings a type of death, yet it is the gateway to life.

Who is on the throne? This is the one question that will never go away while we are still in these bodies. It is a question that serves as a great reminder of our constant need for surrender.

Some of you who are still reading are probably starting to get tired of the message. "Can we not just have some encouragement? This message is so negative."

I agree. To the natural mind, this message of death to the self-life and the idea of entering the kingdom through many afflictions can be a bit disheartening. So, let us insert some of the benefits of allowing ourselves to be squeezed by the Lord.

Incidentally, is it not interesting that the Lord speaks of grapes being crushed, wheat being bruised, precious metal being beaten, and gold being refined by fire?

Why was the Lord so touched by the breaking of an alabaster box and the tears that fell on His feet? That which has been broken is precious to the Lord, and the fragrance of brokenness fills the house of the Lord.

DECENTRALIZATION

Yes, everyone has a fragrance. The spiritual fragrance has nothing to do with shampoo or deodorant. The spiritual fragrance that is sweet to the Lord is the one of brokenness.

Who in the New Testament exudes the greater testimony? Was it the religious men and those with important positions, or was it a woman who was extremely thankful for the forgiveness of her many sins and whose forgiveness caused her to love the Lord with all her heart. She was sensitive to the Lord's considerations because she was broken. Men and women who are not broken just do not have much in the way of sensitivity.

We can know a lot about the Lord. An intellectually superior person can figure out a certain amount of things from Scripture. An academic can add his two cents as well, but the desires of the heart can only be explored by those whose hearts are completely His.

Let us be reminded one more time: You cannot make yourself to be spiritually sensitive any more than you can crucify yourself. You do not have to; you only have to surrender.

> *"The refining pot is for silver and the furnace for gold, but the Lord tests hearts"*
>
> ~**PROVERBS 17:3**

It is precisely that testing from the Lord that works sensitivity and sacrificial love into us. Notice the term sacrificial love, not

THE CROSS IN YOUR PATH

a naturally sweet disposition that we just inherited. The Lord's refining fire burns up the dross, along with its myriads of masks, and allows for a measure of the divine nature to shine through. Spiritual sensitivity can never be imitated. Oh, you could try, but only until the perfect heart test falls on you; then you will want to hide in your room and hope that no one noticed the real you.

How would you rather be known? As one who pretended to be spiritual in the community here on earth or as one who is noticed and known by heavenly-created beings? It is only the work of the cross that will make you spiritually sensitive. The work of the cross gives you more insight into the Lord and the Scriptures, into the purpose of God in creation, and into the purpose of God in man than you could ever obtain by any amount of schooling.

Many, if not most, of the old hymns were written by men and women who had passed through the fires of God's choosing. It was out of loss and heartbreak that they were able to write with a sense of depth. Much that was sung in the past has fallen out of favor. Some of the language seems archaic today, and the message no longer resonates. Perhaps one of the reasons that so many of today's songs are shallow and lack much spiritual substance is simply because experiencing the cross is also unsung.

Taking up your cross and self-denial just do not make for happy, rollicking praise lyrics, do they? Self-expression is a lot more fun ns come across as professional Christians.

than self-denial. Maybe that is why so many professional Christians come across as professional Christians.

Who is really on the throne of your life, your business, your church? It is the work of the cross in your life, and only the work of the cross, that is the perfect surgery for the removal of you from the throne. It is God's chosen method of decentralization.

CHAPTER 11

His Cross at Gethsemane

Everything we will ever know about the cross was first experienced by Jesus Christ. Anything of the cross that we have ever touched, He touched first. You can gain a lot of understanding regarding what to expect from the cross if you understand what happened to Him in His final hours.

First came Gethsemane. Why is this place so important in His history? It is for the same reason that it is important in your own personal story. Gethsemane is the place where a decision is made. It is where one decides whether or not he will accept the circumstances that God has assigned to him. It is the hour of deciding if you will allow the sovereign hand of God to work within your heart. Will you allow or reject it?

THE CROSS IN YOUR PATH

Our Lord Jesus was perfect in every way. He was absolutely sinless, yet His Father deemed there was a work of the cross to be accomplished, even for the sinless One. Obviously, His need was not for salvation, but there was a perfecting work even for the perfect One. "He learned obedience from the things which He suffered" (Hebrews 5:8).

If the Father would choose the cross even for His own pure and sinless Son, then He will surely choose it for you and me. Whenever the cross comes, a Gethsemane will come in some form. Sometimes you are able to pass through the decision process quickly, but at other times, it becomes an agonizing process that seems to last a very long time. In either case, the thing which is discovered is the same. You discover the same thing that your Lord Jesus discovered: natural life does not wish to go to the cross. Divine life is willing; natural life, however, will put up an all-out fight to keep from going there. The final choice will be agonizing, for it demands the denial of human nature and surrendering to divine nature. Oh yes, every reason, logic, and defense mechanism will rise up with a convincing argument as to why the cross is really unnecessary.

It has been said that most people would be willing to accept the cross if they could have it in private and in a controlled atmosphere. Gethsemane would be okay if only we could choose the terms. Of course, then it would not be Gethsemane at all.

CHAPTER 12

Betrayal

After Gethsemane comes betrayal. Of all the wounds in the life of a Christian, betrayal ranks tops in its ability to debilitate and plant a virus of bitterness.

The Lord Jesus was betrayed by one of His very own disciples. We can accept this pretty easily since we already know that Judas was appointed for this very purpose. It is an entirely different matter, however, when the object of betrayal is you. It is bad enough if you are betrayed by someone whom you really do not care for in the first place, but when it is a close friend, or worse yet, a loved one, that is real betrayal. You did not see it coming. It was, in fact, a totally unexpected shock.

A million things flood your mind: "Why did this happen? Is it my fault?" Yet, there is no answer, no satisfying conclusion.

THE CROSS IN YOUR PATH

You are left with the most deafening silence and the emptiest void that you have ever experienced. You feel more alone than you can ever remember. Those first hours are a traumatic time in which your mind is numb. Trauma turns to heartbreak, but the mind is still cloudy. Heartbreak eventually draws back just far enough to make room for lingering disappointment to show up, and you just flop down on the sofa.

If you have been around for very long, you may have already discovered that betrayal has left its ashes all over the world. You were not surprised that it happened to the Lord Jesus, but boy, were you shocked when it happened to you! (If it has not happened to you, be glad and do not go looking for it.)

Throughout history, influential Christians have not often referred to this issue. That is probably a mark of spiritual maturity, but when you read their biographies, you discover that none of them escaped it. Apparently, walking through and overcoming the searing loss of betrayal is part of God's training.

So, the question comes to us again: How will we respond? Let me offer a few choices from the menu at Pity Pantry. The appetizers are anger and resentment. The main course is a big, fat plate of bitterness. (Be warned: If you choose bitterness, no amount of mouthwash will ever remove the bad taste.) For dessert, there is the tempting but unsatisfying bowl of telling everyone in the free world about how badly you have been mistreated. The best choice, of course, is none of the above. In fact, do not even visit the Pity Pantry.

BETRAYAL

You can choose to accept that God has allowed this thing to happen in your life. I know that it seems to be unreasonable and unfair, yet nothing has befallen you, not even this terrible thing, without God's full knowledge and His permission.

It is well known that Andrew Murray once found himself in his very own perfectly timed trial. It seems there was some controversy after one of his messages at a conference in England. When asked by a certain young woman as to how he was handling the difficulty, his thoughtful response was as follows:

> *"First, He brought me here. It is by His will that I am in this straight place. In that fact I will rest. Next, He will keep me here in His love and give me the grace to behave as His child. Then He will make the trial a blessing, teaching me the lessons He intends for me to learn and working in me the grace He means to bestow. Last, in His good time, He can bring me out again. How and when only He knows."*

Andrew chose to entrust himself, along with the accompanying circumstances of his fiery ordeal, into the faithful hands of his Lord. There was not a hint of self-defense or self-pity.

The young woman who had made the initial inquiry was herself in a season of loss and trial. The response that she received took root in her and left what was to become an effectual testimony both in her and later through her. That young woman was Amy Carmichael.

The writers of this book had a relationship with a man from Nepal. He was a humble servant of the Lord and a true apostle.

He was small in stature and a simple man whose quiet presence disguised the fact that he was actually a spiritual giant. In the privacy of our homes, he recounted to us his years in prison and the treatment he had received at the hands of heathen men.

Our dear brother (now gone to be with the Lord) was the first convert in his country. He planted numerous churches throughout the Hindu kingdom of Nepal. His travel was mostly by foot, as Nepal does not have much roadway. He led many people to the Lord.

He was asked what situation in Nepal caused the most suffering. "Was it the terrible conditions in prison or the guards? Was it the dangerous criminals on the paths or even the tigers?"

Without hesitation, he replied, "The pain I have experienced at the hands of Christians who have betrayed me is much more hurtful than any suffering that came to me from the hands of unbelievers."

By the way, our old friend showed not one iota of resentment or bitterness. His spirituality made me feel ashamed of my own lack thereof.

BETRAYAL

These are the testimonies of two of the Lord's servants. One I knew personally; the other I know primarily from his writings. Both of them share a common theme. They both had what we refer to as "no smell of smoke." I am, of course, referring to the Holy Spirit's record of Daniel's friends when they came out of the fiery furnace. The ropes that bound them were the only things consumed in the furnace—nothing else. The furnace is intended to burn up those things that bind us. When they came out, there was no smell of smoke on them.

No smell of smoke is a reference to no anger or bitterness, nor even a memory of mistreatment.

Why is this mentioned? We are all destined for some fiery ordeals. Some folks come out with the odor of smoke all over them, and they keep it with them. Sometimes it is the odor of, "Look what I have been through. See how marvelous my faith was." Other times, the continuous smell keeps announcing all the terrible mistreatments that have been suffered.

Let us take a moment to see how the Lord used His memory of what men did to Him. Did you notice how He cursed those ungodly rascals? Did you hear how He raged against those who drove nails through His hands? Do you remember how He told over and over again about the unfair treatment He received? Did you hear Him repeatedly defending Himself against the lies and accusations made against Him? Did you hear Him mentioning how sorry He felt when His robe was stripped off and a crown of thorns placed on His head?

THE CROSS IN YOUR PATH

No, you did not hear any of that. You should check the record for yourself. He asked God to forgive them. After the Resurrection, our Lord walked, talked, and lived as if the Crucifixion had never even happened. There was no rebuke to the disciples who fled and no replay of the gory details of His agony and suffering.

Following His resurrection, He appeared alongside two disciples as they were walking to Emmaus, but their eyes were prevented from recognizing Jesus. As He spoke with them, their hearts burned within them. There is no indication that the Lord chastised those disciples whose faith was weak. He did not lambast them in this moment of disappointment. He did not even announce Himself, much less testify of His mistreatment. In place of all that, he simply shared something of His nature. He revealed Himself. The testimony of divine nature causes the hearts of men and women to burn within. It is the burn of wonder and glory. Human life loves to complain and insist on vindication, but divine life forgives and encourages forgiveness.

The challenge for you and me is to pass through the furnace of the cross with all of its disappointments, mistreatment, and betrayal, yet come out with no bitterness, no desire for vindication, and no spirit of revenge. Can we believe that God chose a fiery furnace for us in order for these very things that bind our hearts to be consumed? God's plan for us is no smell of smoke—just the fragrance of Christ.

CHAPTER 13

Forgiveness

There is one dimension of the cross in particular that you can rest assured is coming to a neighborhood near you. In fact, it is coming to you personally, and it knows where you live. The opportunity for specific forgiveness will come to every Christian sooner or later. It will also come more than just once or twice. It is interesting, is it not, how much we love to acknowledge the truth that we have been forgiven by the Lord, yet we stiffen up a bit when forgiveness is required of us. It is actually more than a requirement; it is a command.

> *"For if you forgive other people for their offenses, your heavenly Father will also forgive you. But if you do not forgive other people, then your Father will not forgive your offenses"*
> ~MATTHEW 6:14-15

THE CROSS IN YOUR PATH

> *"And his master, moved with anger, handed him over to the torturers until he would repay all that was owed him. My heavenly Father will also do the same to you if each of you does not forgive his brother from your heart"*
>
> **MATTHEW 18:34-35**

The forgiveness that our Lord commands cannot be accomplished as the result of a sweet disposition. In fact, a perfectly orchestrated circumstance will easily unmask that disposition to reveal ugly pride and selfishness. Ouch! So we just need to grit our teeth and use our willpower, right? Wrong! Strength of will does not work; it is not even a good actor.

With all the "how to" stuff available today, there must be a formula that works. Nope. There is no formula that can produce forgiveness from your heart. You will have to deny your right to feel offended. This is a sneaky one. You cannot negotiate with that voice which tells you that you must stand up for your rights, even though it makes a bulletproof argument about the wrong and malice done to you. By the way, it is highly likely that you are in this dilemma in the first place so that the Lord can uncover that proud, self-righteous person inside you who has been masquerading as a spiritual person.

You cannot chase away the spirit of offense by pretending that you are not offended. You overcome that spirit by denying your right to your self-life.

FORGIVENESS

The other thing that will eventually need to die is vindication. This is another slippery little dude who is just waiting for his chance to hit back. Oh, he is willing to let bygones be gone, at least for a while, but sooner or later, he will rebel with a memory full of reminders of what was done. He will also throw in a few exaggerated events at no extra charge. He has been secretly stashing ammo for his moment of revenge. Oh, he will never admit to revenge. He will claim that he is just being honest and speaking the truth in love. Never mind that this little guy does not want you to know your own heart. He is also perfectly happy if you should never come to comprehend the real meaning of "speaking truth in love." This little voice may present a great deal of factual information to your mind. The problem is that he intends the facts for the destruction of relationships rather than for healing. His facts may be undeniable, but his motives stink.

So, how do you overcome this sneaky little liar who wants to lodge in your heart? Well, you deal with him the same way you dealt with the spirit of offense. You do not negotiate or even directly engage him. You mostly deal with yourself by overcoming yourself, but not by self-power or a twelve-step program. For this issue, there is just one step—death—agreeing with the Lord that your victory is in surrender to Him, your Lord and Master. In dying to those things that demand rights, you are surrendering your right to yourself and placing the Lord Jesus on the throne of your heart. This marks the way for forgiveness from your heart.

CHAPTER 14

Before the Collision

―――――∽⋒⋖―――――

Let us take a moment and imagine ourselves on an imaginary version of the Titanic. Let us begin with a supposedly indestructible ship with an experienced captain. Second, throw in a perfectly calm ocean under a beautiful, star-filled night. All seems well. Perhaps you were in the dining room or walking on the deck enjoying the view. Maybe you were snoring away in your comfy cabin. In any case, you had no idea that an iceberg was lurking right smack dab in your path, much less that you were heading full speed for disaster.

The next thing you know, you are jolted from your meal, walk, or sleep. You still have no clue as to what just happened and no earthly idea what is about to happen. Your ship just hit an

THE CROSS IN YOUR PATH

iceberg and knocked a hole in your vessel. Now the unimaginable is about to happen. Your supposedly unsinkable ship is about to get swallowed up and sink out of sight.

Here is a quandary. That iceberg was already there. Of course, most of it was hidden, yet it was there just waiting. You never saw it. Your captain did not see it, either, until it was too late.

Remember, this is intended to be a spiritual story. At this point, you would, at the very least, demand a full refund for the voyage. The person who convinced you to go on this journey clearly oversold it to you. Worse yet, you were never told about this terrible possibility. Maybe you could sue the shipbuilder for shabby work. You would probably reserve most of your anger for the captain. After all, you had trusted his judgment and assumed that his experience would keep you safe. Lastly, you might be one of those who blames God. After all, it was He who placed the iceberg there. He knew the ship was going to collide with the iceberg, yet He did not stop it. Why?

This story of a ship destined for disaster is not as far-fetched as it may seem. You have probably already figured out that the ship in this story could be an assembly of God's people anywhere in the world. It may be your assembly. Almost everyone in church life will sooner or later find himself or herself as a character in this story. Let us break it down.

When your dream of the perfect church gets smashed by something hidden from your previous knowledge, it is so

BEFORE THE COLLISION

shockingly unfair that you cannot help but feel that someone is to blame. When you first came to Christ and initially found the church, it was all so promising. It was even exciting!

Remember? Now, post-trauma, you demand a refund. You had previously testified about your new life with your new spiritual family. Now you present the entire thing as a mistake.

You thought that your ship, your church, or your spiritual family was solid and unsinkable. Now you feel duped and confused. Your leaders (the captain in this story) have failed you. How quickly we can go from laying palm branches before our hero to shouts of "Crucify Him!"

By the way, if you are one of those people who blames God for the iceberg that is sinking your assembly, well, you are actually partially correct. You are also way off course. Yes, God has allowed you to be in this circumstance for His own personal, deeper work in you. You place blame because you do not understand His ways. You are angry because, once again, He did not meet your expectations.

Now, that little story may seem silly to some, but it was not silly for the people on the real Titanic, and it will not seem silly for you, either, when the iceberg of God collides with your life.

Get ready for the cross to cut deeper, and do not forget that it is all part of God's perfect spiritual surgery just for you.

CHAPTER 15

Leaders

Let us return for a moment to those recognized as leaders. One of them was most likely "your guy." After things started going south, you began to hear things about him. Someone felt it was their duty to disclose some information about this man. Some of the information was quite personal. Supposed facts and their logical conclusions began to find their way around.

More and more people began hearing that the man in question had to be guilty of something. Sometimes it is something regarding a moral failure. That kind of thing is a clear-cut issue, but on many occasions, there is no moral issue. There is nothing concrete to attack.

Sometimes, in the midst of a church crisis, a once influential and respected man begins to get stamped with a label that

THE CROSS IN YOUR PATH

shouts, "guilty of this and that." It does not matter what "this and that" are or even if they are true. A person can repent from even a terrible moral failure, but you cannot repent from half-truths, exaggerations, or malicious gossip about you. Elusive accusations are perhaps among the most hurtful things that can ever be hurled at another believer.

Okay, so your captain has failed. A mob is beginning to form. They will not be throwing actual stones; they will most likely be throwing accusations. You, dear reader, will be tempted to join them. The new leaders brought forth will be Mr. Logic and his sidekick, Mr. Legal Analyst. It is a big mistake to underestimate their ability to draw you in. Please do not join. Before you throw your first stone, be sure to know that you cannot take it back. If you contribute to innuendo, you will help spread a virus that never quite goes away.

You should also remember that your one-time skipper has a wife and children. He used to have friends, and you were once named among them.

So, what now? It is not just his crisis; it is yours, too. Again, a heartbreaking disappointment has brought you face to face with your inevitable cross.

NOTE:

Not every disappointment qualifies as the cross; only those events that have been perfectly orchestrated to expose your self-reliance.

LEADERS

This is a season when it is wise to move slowly and conduct one's business in the absolute fear of the Lord. In fact, it is the perfect time to sit at His feet and ask, "Lord, what are You speaking to me? What are You trying to teach me through this?" After all, do you really think that your Lord was ignorant as to what was about to happen? Was He asleep in the boat? I know the whole thing is just not fair. Oh, but where did you ever get the idea that fair was a spiritual term?

Now, let us change gears for a moment as we move on from our obsession with those who are leaders and turn our consideration to the person in the mirror. Let us pretend that you who are reading this are the target of such a catastrophe. Leadership is no longer the issue; you are!

You have been hurt, dismissed, and suffered damage to your personal reputation. Terrible things were spoken about you, but you are still in the atmosphere. Former friends and even loved ones are also wounded. The problem is that they hold you accountable for a big chunk of their troubles. You are now officially the target.

It gets even worse. You discover and then repeatedly discover that there is absolutely nothing you can do to fix this predicament. You are now in a state of social and psychological exile, and your only hope of reinstatement is a miracle. You wish for that miracle to come as soon as possible. You pray for it, yet heaven remains silent. You are alone on an island. There is absolutely no hope anywhere in sight.

THE CROSS IN YOUR PATH

You cannot unscramble eggs and put them back into their shells. You cannot change anyone's thoughts about you. Any attempt to explain yourself will, at best, just fall to earth and, at worst, just add to the confusion.

This grim scenario is exactly the type of thing that has brought many of God's people to a place of resentment, anger, hurt feelings, and, well, I think you get the picture. How will you get off the island of despair? Self-pity makes a lousy raft.

So, what now? Heaven may seem silent, but the Lord is always listening. You see, He has one course for others and another course with your name on it. He knows every single detail of what has happened to you. He allowed it for a purpose.

Only one question is left: Will you allow Him to speak into your broken heart? Will you really allow Him to speak words of correction, discipline, and, yes, encouragement into your deepest parts?

The inevitable cross has come in the perfect way and at the perfect hour for resurrection life to become your very own personal possession. Life out of death was God's plan all along.

CHAPTER 16

Division in the Body of Christ

The very title of this chapter is itself a type of oxymoron, for the very concept of division is a foreign idea to the body of Christ. His body is, or at least should be, the expression of His own mind. Since there is no division whatsoever in the Godhead, why should there be any here? The outflow of Christ's life through His people on earth should actually be the corporate expression of divine mind. Every local assembly that is under His headship is intended to be a local expression of His very nature and personality.

So, how can there possibly be division in the corporate expression of Christ's own body? After all, we have already been forewarned not to be surprised at the fiery ordeal that comes upon us for our testing, as though something strange was happening.

The problem is that the division that strikes close to home comes not only as a surprise but closer to shock and awe.

It has been said that there is no single event in the life of a Christian assembly that causes more damage, deeper wounds, bigger scars, or more lasting hurts than division. The interesting thing about a problem between any two Christians is that it will likely not stay confined to them, even if they try to keep it only between them.

When you first hear about a conflict or disagreement, you probably think that this is just something they will have to work out between themselves. You have no idea that you are about to become an unwilling player in the drama. Why? Because these two folks have spouses, children, and close friends. They also have a few churchmates who have always been slightly suspicious of their motives. People are going to slowly but surely begin to take sides. And guess what? You are one of those people.

"Our side is right. Our friend is better. Bla bla bla." Not only that, but we must do something; we must get involved in this dispute and find a settlement. That is a great idea, Aristotle, except for one small detail: sometimes there is no settlement, no coming together, not even an agreement to disagree. Sometimes, when the dust settles, there are only hurt feelings,

DIVISION IN THE BODY OF CHRIST

bitterness, anger, frustration, finger-pointing... well, you get the picture.

As to that supposed responsibility that you felt to get involved, it was, at best, a presumption but probably just pride. You may have just thrown something into the pot of stew without really knowing what it was. It might even have been something poison.

You think that you must do something. Actually, you are right in that there is something which must be done. The thing is, it is not what first popped into your mind. What really needs to be done is to die to your right to your opinion. I am suggesting your need of death to the self-life in this very matter.

Choosing to die to your rights is never a matter of deciding between right and wrong; it is not logic; it is not coming up with a great solution that will ensure that everyone lives happily ever after. The need is to hear the Lord's voice in the heat of the moment, and that, dear friend, will not happen if you are not ready to surrender. "Surrender what exactly?" you ask. I cannot define your personal "exactly what," but I can offer a few possibilities.

The aftermath of a church split is no laughing matter. Some of the wounded will never recover. Some will say that the pain of disappointment is just too great, and they will never again take the risk of being disappointed. Some will give up completely on the idea of corporate life and decide that it just cannot work. Some will be careful not to blame God; they will just insist that the problem is people and that people will never agree. All of these dear folks actually have the same thing in common: they all met the cross with a perfectly premeasured portion of disappointment and heartbreak. The Lord Jesus turned out to be someone other than whom they had expected.

Are you willing to surrender to disappointment without becoming bitter? Are you willing to surrender the loss of a friend because you did not take his side? Are you willing to be misunderstood? Are you willing to endure criticism and, worse yet, innuendo?

No one is able to use even the strongest human will to go through these things. You can only ask the Lord to speak to your heart and protect you from leading by your natural life.

There is no cute formula for victory here. There is only the continuous seeking of a soft heart and the inner voice that says, "Wait for Me."

It is humanly impossible to be still and wait when you feel like a paper cup in a hurricane, but thankfully, human possibility is not the only option. The reality of divine life does not come forth overnight, and it does not come by magic. You have His life within you, and now you are learning how to live by it as you walk through seemingly impossible circumstances. Your Lord has chosen those circumstances just for you, and as you pass through them, you will find both a bigger Christ and a different Christ than the one you had expected. Yes, He turns out to be different than any of us envisioned. You see, He never intended to allow us to relate to Him only by the limitations of our childlike mind. He saved us with the full intention of bringing us all the way into the deepest possible fellowship with Him, spirit to Spirit, with nothing in between.

CHAPTER 17

The Precious Waste

Everyone who continues on the path of transformation will likely hear the following message: "Why this waste?" It is a message that will come to you directly from the hearts and lips of other believers. You may be surprised to learn the origin of this message and even shocked as to the identity of its first preachers.

The scene is a banquet. The Lord Jesus is there, along with His disciples and the host. A certain woman, upon learning that her Lord was present, makes her unannounced entry. She has brought an alabaster vial of very expensive perfume. She took her life savings and poured it out, and in so doing, she anointed the Lord with something of great value.

Now, you might expect the crowd at the banquet to reward such a woman and her sacrificial act with a standing ovation, but instead she received a message that would be repeated down through the centuries: "Why this waste?"

Who would have the cold audacity to respond this way? Well, it was none other than the Lord's disciples. There is more. They were indignant toward this woman. In other words, they held this woman in contempt and rejected her gift as being misguided. We would expect such a response from Judas, but not from the others.

Well, before we get too upset with the disciples, we need to consider a matter of spiritual significance. The disciples were not yet "spiritual men." They had not yet met their own inevitable cross. They did not know their own hearts. As such, they could only judge things from an outward and natural perspective. They did not realize that they were only *natural* men who could not yet discern the *spiritual*. They could only think from a human perspective, such as, "We could have sold this perfume and used the money to buy more tracts or Bibles or sponsor a picnic for the poor."

Let us look at the response of the Lord Jesus. His response to those present was that this woman had done a good thing because she had done it *to Him*. The Lord, right then and there, gave the *divine life* answer to the *natural life* question of "Why this waste?" The Lord disclosed to all who were able to hear that there is a difference between doing something for Him versus doing something to Him. Furthermore, the Lord pointed out that she had anointed His body in preparation for

THE PRECIOUS WASTE

His burial. By her act of sacrifice and her spiritual affection, this woman also gave a message that will be shouted into eternity. You see, our Lord judges matters from the perspective of resurrection life rather than human logic. Service unto Him is higher than service for Him.

"What is the difference?" you ask. Ministry and the love of ministry have sidetracked many a Christian from nearness to the Lord. It is so easy to feel good about one's Christian service and to actually love that feeling even more than you love the Lord Himself: "I am just so happy that I am fulfilling the ministry that God has given me as a missionary, a pastor, a praise leader, a counselor, a Sunday school teacher" . . . and you can add your own thing to this list.

Yes, we tend to be quite satisfied with the ministries that He has given us. That is understandable.

Now, here is a dilemma. Suppose the same God who gave you a ministry now asks you to lay it down. Can you walk away? Maybe, but probably not. Men will fight like medieval warriors to keep their work, their lifestyle, and especially their reputation. The reason that men fight so hard for the preservation of these things is because they are so important, and if they fail, the kingdom will suffer. The kingdom will suffer all right, but whose kingdom?

Again, if God asks you to lay down something that is so bonded to your self-identity, can you do it?

THE CROSS IN YOUR PATH

Many men and women gave themselves to the Lord in their youth with hearts to serve Him. Some of them went on to seminary and eventually became pastors and, in some cases, missionaries or even leaders of religious organizations. These folks all had something in common at the beginning of their journey—a desire to serve the Lord. Now, decades later, some of them have another thing in common. It is that the cost of preserving their position, lifestyle, and reputation has slowly but surely replaced a heart for the Lord with a life of entanglements.

Those men, along with their wives, children, and organizations, would have been better served had they simply laid down their ministry to know the Lord. Of course, they know the Lord as Savior, but do they really know Him?

Does this sound harsh?

No one, whether a pastor, a missionary, or the head of a religious organization, can truly serve the Lord until their love for Him surpasses their love of ministry. This is actually a fundamental spiritual truth. To know Him is the highest call; all else is just traffic on life's highway. The love of ministry and its sense of accomplishment are often the mirage that detours from spiritual intimacy.

It is important to recall the Lord's response to that which others saw only as waste. He said that it was a good act because it was done to Him in preparation for His burial. It is so easy for His response to sail over our heads. "Preparation for My burial" is not a matter of anything morbid. It is an issue of

THE PRECIOUS WASTE

spiritual reality. There cannot be a burial without a death—no death, no burial, and, therefore, no resurrection.

When something deemed precious is poured out on the Lord, others may only see waste, while the Lord sees something much deeper. While others might even be angry, the Lord Jesus is actually blessed in a way that is beyond human articulation. The affection of one grateful woman for her Lord more than answers the question of "Why this waste?" In fact, it was such a blessed thing to our Lord that He right then and there declared before all that this woman's sacrifice was to be a permanent portion of the gospel.

What is sacrifice?

If I took a bottle of my wife's perfume and poured it out in the backyard, would that be a sacrifice? No, it would only be an act of religious drama. There is no benefit to the Lord here. The sacrifice that is pleasing to God is the one that is requested by His still, small voice. It is not the thing that you decided you could live without. It is the costly thing. Sacrifice is in His asking and your surrender.

The ultimate sacrifice is your self-life. After all, it is the most precious thing that you possess. You see, your heart just might be the alabaster box. Will you allow it to be broken for Christ?

The Final Word

It is probable that you began your Christian life with a very limited gospel. Perhaps we all did. Maybe, just maybe, someone should have told us that within our glorious salvation experience, an exceedingly wicked heart still lurked. This is, of course, the great Christian paradox. How can a person who has been washed clean by the blood of Christ still be in possession of a deceitful heart? Well, God knows the answer to that question, and He knows exactly how to bring things into the right relationship.

We were born again, yet we still have one severe spiritual handicap. Spiritual problems require a spiritual solution. At the very beginning of our new life in Christ, it would probably have been helpful if someone had told us that a measure of suffering and disappointment was just around the corner. (We probably would not have believed it anyway.) Someone should have also mentioned that we were only at stage one, not the finish line. If only we had known of the many crossroads that lay ahead,

THE CROSS IN YOUR PATH

maybe we could have been better prepared, but probably not. You see, we had to become broken. We had to become convinced of our absolute need for that brokenness. That convincing takes time, perhaps an entire lifetime.

There are plenty of issues along the course of life about which you do not have a say. There are circumstances in which you do not get a vote or even the release of constructive criticism.

Life has you hedged in. Here comes another crossroad, another decision, another choice. Dear Christian, this is where you do get to make a choice and you do have a say. In the midst of trying and seemingly unfair circumstances, there is a choice to be made, and you are the only one who can make it. It is your choice. You can choose to be a victim of these circumstances (and that is probably what you will do unless you believe that Jesus Christ is on His throne and in charge of all that has happened to you). Or, you can choose to take the higher road. You can agree with Him and choose His ground. You can now choose the cross.

Now you see—really see—with new eyes that His way is always the higher way, always the way of the cross.

www.ingramcontent.com/pod-product-compliance
Lightning Source LLC
Chambersburg PA
CBHW030528080526
44586CB00011B/358